4.1

ZENA SCHOOL LIBRARY

KANGAROOS

AUSTRALIAN ANIMAL DISCOVERY LIBRARY

Lynn M. Stone

Rourke Corporation, Inc.
Vero Beach, Florida 32964

© 1990 Rourke Corporation, Inc.

All rights reserved. No part of this book
may be reproduced or utilized in any form
or by any means, electronic or mechanical
including photocopying, recording or by any
information storage and retrieval system
without permission in writing from the
publisher.

PHOTO CREDITS

All photos © Lynn M. Stone

ACKNOWLEDGEMENTS

The author thanks the following for photographic assistance:
Fleays Fauna Centre, West Burleigh, Queensland, Australia;
Lone Pine Koala Sanctuary, Brisbane, Queensland, Australia;
Queensland National Parks and Wildlife Service; Blue Mountains
Tourism Authority, Katoomba, Australia

LIBRARY OF CONGRESS
Library of Congress Cataloging-in-Publication Data
Stone, Lynn M.
    Kangaroos / by Lynn M. Stone.
    p. cm. — (Australian animal discovery library)
    Summary: Describes the habitat, lifestyle, infancy, predators,
relationship with humans, and future of this well-known
Australian animal.
  ISBN 0-86593-058-9
    1. Kangaroos—Juvenile literature. [1. Kangaroos.]
I. Title. II. Series: Stone, Lynn M. Australian animal discovery
library.
QL737.M35S75   1990
599.2—dc20   90-30486
                                   CIP
                                   AC

TABLE OF CONTENTS

The Kangaroo	5
The Kangaroo's Cousins	6
How They Look	9
Where They Live	11
How They Live	14
The Kangaroo's Babies	16
Predator and Prey	19
The Kangaroo and People	20
The Kangaroo's Future	22
Glossary	23
Index	24

THE KANGAROO

The long-tailed, bounding kangaroo is probably the best known of all Australian animals.

Kangaroos are pouched animals, or **marsupials.** A mother kangaroo uses her pouch to hold her baby.

Australia has 54 different kinds, or **species,** of kangaroos. Some of them are known as wallabies, wallaroos, and other names.

Kangaroos run as if they are on steel springs. They bound on big, powerful hind legs at up to 40 miles per hour.

A big kangaroo cannot leap over a tall building, but it can cover 40 feet in a single bound!

Wallaby helping baby into pouch

THE KANGAROO'S COUSINS

The family of kangaroos is quite large. The well-known big kangaroos are closely related to wallaroos and many of the large wallabies.

Several groups of smaller kangaroos are more distant relatives of the big 'roos. These smaller animals include the rat kangaroos, hare wallabies, pademelons, tree kangaroos, and others.

Most of the kangaroo species live in Australia. A few live in New Guinea, an island north of Australia.

Tree Kangaroo

HOW THEY LOOK

The kangaroo's long tail helps it spring upward and sit upright. The big hind feet are great for bounding, and the small "hands" are used to comb fur and pick up food.

Kangaroos are furry creatures with long ears, like rabbits, and big, dark eyes, like deer.

The biggest 'roos are the red and two species of gray. Big males can weigh 150 pounds and stand nose to nose with a man. The smallest species are the size of rabbits.

Kangaroos are generally tan, gray, or reddish brown. Wallabies have similar colors, but they often have white trim.

Eastern Gray Kangaroo

WHERE THEY LIVE

Kangaroos and wallabies of one kind or another live throughout Australia.

Scientists call these bounding marsupials **macropods.** Macropod means "big foot," and kangaroos have done very well with their big feet.

Kangaroos' big feet have taken them into many different kinds of homes, or **habitats.** Some types live on rugged wooded mountainsides. Others live in rocky places, deserts, and the hot, rainy forests of northern Australia.

Almost every habitat in Australia has one or more kangaroo species.

Wallaby habitat: Blue Mountains National Park, New South Wales

Pretty-faced Wallaby cleaning paws

Red Kangaroo nursing

HOW THEY LIVE

Kangaroos are mostly **nocturnal.** Nocturnal animals are active at night rather than during the day.

Some species of kangaroos travel alone. Others, such as the eastern gray kangaroo, travel in groups called **mobs.**

Mobs of eastern gray kangaroos are usually made up of females and their babies.

Many species of kangaroos which feed together don't spend the day together.

Male kangaroos sometimes fight with each other over females. Most of the fighting is done with kicks.

Eastern Gray Kangaroo

THE KANGAROO'S BABIES

Kangaroos have one baby at a time, but they often have more than one baby in a year. Baby kangaroos are called joeys.

The red kangaroo is among the biggest kangaroos. At birth, however, a baby red kangaroo weighs less than one ounce.

A baby kangaroo lives in its mother's pouch for up to eight and one-half months.

The large species of kangaroos become adults at about two years of age.

A captive red kangaroo lived to be 22 years.

Eastern Gray joey

PREDATOR AND PREY

Kangaroos are plant eaters. In some areas almost all of their food is grass.

Like other plant-eating animals, kangaroos are **prey,** or food, for hunting animals.

Animals that hunt other animals for food are **predators.** The main predator of kangaroos is the dingo, Australia's wild dog.

Eagles also take a few small kangaroos. On the Australian island of Tasmania, the Tasmanian devil eats wallabies now and then.

Eastern Gray Kangaroo grazing

THE KANGAROO AND PEOPLE

Visitors to Australia love the kangaroos. Many Australians love kangaroos, too. Others aren't fond of 'roos.

Kangaroos eat the same food that sheep and cattle eat: grass. Because of that, some species of kangaroos are **pests** to farmers.

Where they are pests, kangaroos can be shot by kangaroo hunters. In 1989, Australian kangaroo hunters were free to shoot nearly 4 million kangaroos. The government decides how many kangaroos can be killed.

Australia ships some of the kangaroo fur, skin, and meat to other countries. The meat is sold for both humans and pets.

Eastern Gray Kangaroo male

THE KANGAROO'S FUTURE

New farms with their crops and water holes for farm animals have helped the large species of kangaroos. The change from forest to farm, however, has hurt some of the small species. These little kangaroos are not hunted.

For now, most of the kangaroo species are common in Australia. Eighteen million people live in Australia. The country probably has far more kangaroos than people. One thing is for sure: there are too many kangaroos to count!

Glossary

habitat (HAB a tat)—the kind of place an animal lives in, such as desert

macropod (MAAH crow pohd)—any of the various kinds of kangaroos

marsupial (mar SOOP ee ul)—a family of mammals in which females have a pouch for raising the young, which are born not fully formed

mob (MAAHB)—a group of kangaroos

nocturnal (nohk TUR nal)—active at night

pest (PEHST)—an animal whose activities or presence is not wanted

predator (PRED a tor)—an animal that kills other animals for food

prey (PRAY)—an animal that is hunted by another for food

species (SPEE sheez)—within a group of closely related animals, one certain kind

INDEX

age 16
babies 16
color 9
ears 9
eyes 9
feet 5, 9, 11
fighting 14
food 19, 20
future 22
habitat 11
hands 9
height 9
hunting of 20

kangaroo, gray 9, 11
         rat 6
         red 9, 16
         tree 6
leap 5
macropod 11
marsupial 5
meat 20
mob 14
pademelon 6
pouch 5, 16
predator 19
tail 5, 9
wallabies 5, 6, 9
wallaroos 5, 6
weight 9